noonaD

noona
by
januarieYork

Foreword by
Gabrielle Patterson

VK PRESS
Indianapolis, IN

VK Press, LLC
PO BOX 78044
Indianapolis, IN 46278
www.vkpresses.com

Copyright © 2021 by januarieYork

All rights reserved. No part of this book may be reproduced or transmitted in any form or by any means, graphic, electronic, or mechanical including photocopying, recording, taping or by any information storage and retrieval system, without the written permission of the publisher, except where permitted by law.

If you would like to do any of the above, please seek permission first by contacting VK Press, LLC.

Editors: Amanda Wolf and Rohini Townsend
Copyeditor: Tamara Hibbler
Cover and Interior Design: Sylvia "ess mckee" Rivers

Library of Congress Control Number: 2019908539

First edition published June 29, 2021 in the United States by VK Press, LLC

E-Book ISBN 978-0-9982754-7-5
Paperback ISBN 978-0-9982754-8-2

Have you ever picked up a book, read the dedication, and wondered if it was a book for you? Have you ever sat a book down based on the dedication(s)? I have but I can be strange sometimes. Nonetheless, this is the reason I broke the rules and placed my dedications in the back. I wanted every woman that reads this book to experience it as if it was written solely for them with no precursor. It is my hope that by the time you reach the end, you will have become so connected to some of the stories and poems found here that you will use the blank line at the end to add your name to the list. This is as much for YOU as it is for me, as it is for every woman.

Contents

Foreword	9
Prologue	11
The Ice Skater	13

Chapter One: Blood Orange — 15

Nomad Ramblings: Somewhere,	16
Life Lines	19
dawndusk	20
C. U. N.(ext) T.(uesday)	21
The Butterfly Effect	23
Air Max 10s	24
Saliva	26
Sex	27
Money Shot Ramblings: Somewhere,	29
Yin Yang Ramblings: Somewhere,	32

Chapter Two: Compromise for What? — 35

AlbuquerQUEEN Ramblings: Somewhere,	36
Skeletons	38
Crash…	39
Compromise	40
Look In Fly	41
Love Ramblings: Somewhere,	43
DNR Order	47
PenmanShit	48
Live from the Comedy Theater	50
Destruction I	51
Richard	53
Cryola	56
Sugar Daddy	57
Destruction II	58
…Test Dummies	59
Eight Hundred Two Seven Three, Eight Two Five Five	62

Chapter Three: The Edge of the Cliff — 65
    Scattered Brain — 66
    A Familiar Name — 67
    Surgery Ramblings: Somewhere, — 70
    Kintsugi — 72
    Missou — 73
    Edge of the Cliff — 74
    3 AM Musing — 75
    Strength Ramblings: Somewhere, — 77
    Junkie Shyt — 79
    7 A.M. — 80
    Ghost Zaddy — 81
    Stuff — 82

Chapter Four: The eXquisite Pain, 3463 — 87
    EL oh EL — 88
    Word Ramblings: Somewhere, — 89
    (T)HugzMansion — 90
    Check Ya'self Que(EN) — 91
    Stuff II — 93
    Jill Ramblings: Somewhere, — 94
    Eugene Street — 98
    eXquise, mi Amor — 99
    BaDFucKiNdeCisIonS — 100
    The Chrysalis — 103
    Put a Wing on It: Rambling from El Matador Beach — 104
    WYFS — 106
    The (RE)Tired Red Cape: Rambling from the Lido Deck — 109

EpiloVe — 112
Affirmational Ingredient List — 114
Dedications — 116
    Intergalactic, Unapologetically Black Women I Know — 118
Final Thought: Somewhere, — 120
About the Author — 121

Gabrielle Patterson

"When are you going to get some new tennis shoes?"

    I'm referring to white Reebok classics (the cute, girly kind). The kind girls wore with tennis skirts or fresh white shorts back in the day. This is a question I often asked Kendria.

    Who am I? I'm her sister, her bestie, her advisor, and adversary all rolled up into one. I know her ***well***. Which is why I often teased her about those tennis shoes. I'm Gabrielle from back in the day. To me, she's little sis. Today, you might know her as the Queen of Fashion. The girl whose style breaks boundaries in our small (big) town. I know the girl who knew how to get the most out of a pair of tennis shoes: Reebok Classics to be exact.

    However, that was before her metamorphosis; before the modeling and before the *celebrity*.

    You might know her simply as *"nSay"*, *"Januarie,"* or maybe even *"Ms. Smith."* I know her as "why don't you do that poem about (insert topic) and let the world know what I know?! Like how crazy [and] hilarious, or how diverse you really are! How you didn't really let him get away with that bullshit. He's somewhere immortalized in a notebook with catchy rhymes and staccato rhythm, but he might not ever show his face again after this one!"

    Oh yeah! I was always egging her on. Debauchery is my middle name! But she would always be like, "Nah, I'ma do something else" or "I can't do that" even when I could see she wanted to. I knew it could be therapeutic and that a legion of women would cheer her on, and together we would all march down one main Avenue to his house and---

    But, that wasn't her style.

    Her style is eccentric in every way. Outside the norm. She will internalize what happens around her or from her perch inside a window, capture it, and reshape it into stories on paper painted beautifully and strategically. Her visions are retold from the soul of an empath; someone vulnerable all the time.

Someone who feels everything.

That's what this book is. I call it the "Stories of an Empath." Open and honest. Uncomfortable truth. A sermon of experience. A journey incomplete, but sharing where we've been so far. She and I have been down dark alleyways together, and around every corner we discovered something new, but every time I stopped, I would see her levitate above her space, ascending to another level of her quest to understand why things are the way they are, and putting them to paper. I always wanted her to share those things with you. She always said she would but never did. Until now!

Now you have the rare opportunity to peek inside the mind of a woman who has a little insecurity, a little bit of sass, a little bit of a little girl, and a whole lot of love. You get to know what I know. Congratulations!!!

Take your time with this journey.

Soak it in. When you think you understand it, read it again. I guarantee you will find something different every time. I sure did. These poems are magical if you let them be that for you so take notes.

This book isn't just her story, it's all of ours.

You can find yourself in it AND,

you can find ....yourself, in it.

Thank me later. Never mind, you already bought the book, so get started!!!

What are you waiting for?

Gabrielle Patterson

Prologue

The Street My Heart Paved

My heart is a highway of wander. There are roadmaps available that would allow for easy access, but they've grown old and crinkled in their pages, and the ink has worn away; no one ever uses them. Most people have gone for it on their own accord, leaving behind staggered footprints and dust storms driven away only by the tears I've shed for growth. My heart has landmines waiting to be tripped and stone monuments that depict fallen, phony heroes that once sat at the throne of my love story of the moment. I've basted lies with the honey from between my thighs and cried secretly while washing dishes. My prayers have been desperate enough to request the breaking of soul ties. I've wasted time, energy and plans on false starts and it's hard not to take it all personally when your precious resources begin to feel depleted. Oh, the glasses you'll pour! I knew my well was running low when I entered the last relationship I was in, which in hindsight, was a good reason not to get involved with anyone. But I was smitten with his seemingly eagerness to make me happy and for once, I felt like someone was pouring back into me. Like many times before, I hopped the fence and skipped down a hill of temporary tulips that soon turned a field of yellow dandelions peppered with ants crawling around for a pollen sample. I sneeze at the memory. It wasn't long before I realized I was empty and expected to keep pouring while he was drinking and storing what he had for himself…or other women. This heart of mine has fostered too many lost little boys wearing adult pants that they couldn't properly fit into. They've sought refuge in the guardianship of any companion willing to fly in and clear their runways for takeoff. I've been that person so much that now my brakes squeal like the A-train to Manhattan. In order to fix the insanity, I must look inward.

It is from this street, the street my heart built, that I write. This highway of wander and lust separated yet running parallel and congruently.
This brick road is where I scribe the songs my muses have left behind.

These poems and reflections wander through the avenues that have stamped their names on my chest using my own blood. Here you will find more questions than answers and more hindsight than heeded-instinctive warnings. This isn't just the glass of lemonade. This book is the ingredients list, the trip to the store and the handpicking of the lemons off a tree hanging over a California fence. Towns full of manipulation and hard penises will be urban explored in sonnets. Results and revelations will be revealed in essays that redefine what a rest stop is. I hope this book serves as a reminder not to lose yourself looking for or being in love. I realize the biggest common denominator inside of these mini movies in poetic form is me, therefore, this is not an indictment or declaration of guilt on anyone. Truth is not a friend seeker or a coddler so if ye' seeketh the latter, stop here. *nomaD* is a map through my love experiences that have led me to a heightened awareness and altitude of self.

Thank you for hopping on this plane with me. Every seat is a window. Relax your back and let the natural light come through. (Locate my profile on Spotify and search for the "1000 Miles" playlist; that's the JY-curated soundtrack to this book.) There will be some turbulence, minor bumps and at times, it may look like we are turning around and headed in the wrong direction. Don't worry, it all works out in the end. Oh, and don't be alarmed if we are close to the mountains. It's just so you can see the flags I planted on the many I've conquered. I hope this book helps you conquer some of your own.

I love you.

The Ice Skater

I watched a man ice skate on television
with his partner in his grip
Enthralled with fascination, I stared beyond the music of the
melody that he spun to,
and listened to the heartbeats they created over ice flooring.
He moved with a precise awareness
His knees stiff and balancing his thigh strength with his ankle twists
Silver blades on white boots cut the ice and threw bits of it towards
the speed of light.
He turned
and with his partner in his grip
lifted her over his shoulders while spinning against the gravity
of love
She,
his enigma for the moment
became an unbreakable doll,
flipped in three hundred and sixty degrees of splendor
before being pushed passed masculine shoulders
    180° over head,
then spun into a dance where hands reach for each other's
attention.
As they paralleled with the wind, their eyes acted as road maps
directing their final chords even when the travel was backwards.
He never once dropped her.
Or slipped on his own forgetfulness.
His ego can't be found on the ice,
It's far too cold to be so self-conscious,

So he believes
in himself.
And his hips break the rules of men before him as they grind side to side and his smile begins to widen the space his pride takes up.
This is ice sculpting at its finest.
He is the keeper of the stock and the owner of this land.
His alignment with the soundtrack was worth paying attention to.
He wore enough confidence for them both so
even if they were to touch the ground in accident,
his resolve would have her in an upright spin that it made it all look pre-planned.
The ice skater moved the crowd's applauding hands
His partner slid between his legs
and he scooped her with the flick of his right wrist
Left arm extended, palms up,
Facing heaven.
He pulls energy from the Sun and two become one in front of hundreds.
Flowers are thrown at their feet,
but he knows the biggest bloom in the room is his partner
in his grip
His fingers clench tighter around her hand,
and she smiles,
Then they both bow before the crowd
and skate off in search of their future.

Chapter One:
Blood Orange

"Niggas will piss in your morning smoothie and call it a Probiotic for your PH balance.

Don't drink that shit."

Nomad Ramblings: Somewhere, at an East Coast Rest Stop...

How do heterosexual women who were not exposed to a father (in-home or away) learn to love the opposite sex? It's the same for heterosexual men who lack mothers; how are they to know how to care for a woman? Date a guy with mother issues, and you will find he is just as volatile and emotionally inconsistent as women with father troubles. Then there are the people who grew up with no parents for a variety of reasons, all occurring at no fault of their own.

All these single people are learning through DIY methods on each other. *If you learn how to love based on your experiences, then who you are experiencing love with matters a great deal. And if that is true, then you must be selective in who you learn from or at least scrutinize the lesson. Otherwise, you risk contracting some of the same habits and traits as the dishonorable people you have been exposed to.*

Loving someone goes far beyond dates, public displays of affection, and showing up for what one deems momentous moments. I mean, anyone can smile for the camera when the awards are being passed out. Loving another person involves being cognizant of the type of love you are providing. When is the last time you've personally checked yourself on the love you were presenting your partner? Think about how you deal with opposition within the relationship. Is your communication sufficient? Are your values in alignment with your partner's? Loving someone is an extensive list of checks and balances, and I wonder if that's why they say relationships are hard? I've looked at love with such high regard that I never stopped to question if what I was putting out had any defects. But maybe that's the key to learning how to love correctly. The right person will challenge you in such a way that it will naturally reveal for you the areas that you need to grow in. Dig that term "naturally"; I wrote it that way for a reason. You know what's not natural? Letting an argument be the time you decide to list out all your grievances with each other. All that will yield is a game of tit-for-tat. Hardly any real healthy results will occur from anger, insults, and finger-pointing.

You have to let people naturally evolve into who they are going to be, and we have to be able to focus on ourselves rather than what the other person is missing or not bringing to the table. Growth in relationships doesn't occur because someone issued an ultimatum. Reminding someone of their title (role) as a way of suggesting who they need to be isn't going to get the job done. You don't mature as a girlfriend; you mature as a woman and thus as a mate. The same goes for men. He becomes a better husband because he becomes a better man FIRST. Here's the million-dollar baby: personal, individual growth equates to growth of all things attached to you, including your relationships.

Our ego suggests if the other person isn't meeting our current demand of the month, then we don't have to meet theirs. Higher self tells us that it doesn't matter what they aren't doing – you either let them go or you remain true to who you are and how you love while doing the proper examinations on self to properly assess what needs to happen next. That energy matching shit only makes things more miserable for everyone.

You can't get someone to challenge your love until you are ready to receive that challenge. I'm guessing the more you transcend, the more you open yourself up to others who have peaked at that higher level of self as well. In a less than perfect but possible world, this will lead to your one person, if that's your thing. If not, then at least the pool feels more like the waters you think you should be swimming in. Assessing how you love means crashing headfirst back into your past and finding out who you took your lessons from. Who made you believe $X = Y$? Were they ever logical? Do you love from a place of survival? Does your love come from an absence of some sort: father, brother, dominant male figure? What makes you believe you give healthy love, and how can you validate those beliefs?

In the end, I think every relationship we are in challenges us somehow. It's easier to feel victimized in some instances than it is to look inward and see what you can improve on for the next time. But everyone teaches us something. I guess you could say I've collected good and bad ideas about love and until recent years, never stopped to consider how much of it was tainted. Loving other people is a lesson far too many people are learning through trial and error. Imagine the changes in our society overall if we practiced intentional teaching and continuous learning about what love is, what it isn't, and how to navigate the middle. Personally, I've loved from places of loss, survival, and recovery, and that is no longer the love I want or am willing to give out. I'm now learning how to love people spiritually, from the higher region of myself, and less influenced what Sigmund Freud might call my "superego."

In the event I do have a King out there for me, he won't find me perfect, but I will be better.

Life Lines

What if a thousand first nights came alive in our palms when we placed them together?

dawndusk

But, but -

it just seems so unjust

that the morning would start out two planets away

and the night

would end

without us.

C. U. N.(ext) T.(uesday)

Men,

are always trying…

They push hard as if I were a revolving door-

STUCK-

on its steel axis.

In need of oiling, and their hands the perfect mechanic;

Lubed and ready to make me move.

They *expect* me to move.

They use words

like black magic.

Sifted through once pearly white teeth, now tinted

in Swisher Sweets, *how many licks does it take til' you get to the center of the bold face lie?*

They keep a jazz sonnet deep in their throats, and they scat around

my hope with no bridge like their heart is a Cold tra(i)ne on flames.

Their eyes,

itching to blink and view me from behind…

Pretending to lock with mine but I know that look. They see

through my skin as if transparency were my ethnicity.

It's sickening

how hard they try just to get inside of me.

Does this sound pretentious of me?

Because I've witnessed it. Lived it,

and called it my life; a lost track from

Mary's 94 release.

They flaunt love like a cuff-link

on their t-shirt sleeve:

Blood Orange

on the wrong

shirt,

worn at the wrong time, loosely fitting on me.

And their eagerness,

Bless their hearts of romaine,

wrapped around their faces like clipped foreskin,

keeps their cheekbones up high.

They're almost childlike in their non-innocence,

smiling and shit.

Do they believe I am here to collect their souls? (I think so).

Do they believe I am here to collect their souls?

(But the answer is NO!)

Am I here to collect their souls? (God are you listening?)

Do I believe that I am here to collect their souls?

Do they believe I am here to collect their souls?

Do I believe that I am here to collect their souls?

…to collect their souls?

Do they believe I am here to-…

…..to collect their souls?

Do they….Do I…..believe ----

These men

Who are always trying to get inside of me, but not into me

---do we believe…that I am here

 to collect their fuckin souls?

The Butterfly Effect

If we keep on like this,
sparks gon' lie...
sky gon' crumble...
Somebody is gonna tussle
over someone else's mind control.

Air Max 10s

This isn't for the faint at heart
or the hurry on foot
I'm looking for a book
to be written across my chest in ink that
doesn't fade or hide.
Speak a truth that suggests my every breath,
at each second of impact
entices you to live louder.
I am not to be handled
with rough hands,
full of blisters from
holding baggage too tight.
I'm not to be loved through unbalanced chakras in
need of acknowledgement.
I'm delicate.
There is no other option but to treat me like an orchid.
I need uninterrupted light and sun smiles.
Spring water and a cool space. Gentle touches,
especially when I'm not in bloom.
I seek no illusions of bliss.
No shining knight or white horses,
there's no fairy in my dreams.
Just a library of encyclopedias dedicated to _____,
And I.
A co-author, who will write his name on the line,
hesitating only to make sure his ink is permanent.
And black.   *Black love.*

Shared with the one who will stay the course
of the evolution of us;
Nurtured individually and
by nature, together.
It's not for the faint at heart or the one in the running shoes.

Blood Orange

Saliva

Please excuse this awkward silence.
My tongue is trying not to fumble my words.
My lips are trying not to fondle your mouth.
It's a messy situation.
So just keep talking.
I'll get something figured out.

Sex
Flip flop tan lines,
pointed north,
tip toeing across bedroom skies;
Toes clenched.
Deepness resides in the inside.
Brown legs,
triangularly circling waist.
Wait-
Get a better grip!
Hips don't pie…
3:14 in the AM and hands,
reach for something to tug.
Ungloving fitted caps for mattresses.
Unraveling the thread count.
Pillows topping faces.
Keep traveling south.
Words sound good this way.
Wet weapons grace lips with ease.
Quick tease of eye dances with wolves.
Sheep clothing on the floor.
Moan language.
Name requests.
Outside craniums buried into chest.
This is where the squirt quenches,
the thirst…
Bench press this bohemian body rhapsody.
Catch the motions in the room,
Spinning.
This is why fans stay on.
Sweaty.
This is why palms sing songs.
Finger interlocks.
Effeminate hands trace walls.
Heavy bass in voice,
asking questions for spontaneous choices.

Yes, you can!
Change is cumin'!
Splash cashing in on tongues
tasting each other
having tasted each other,
tasting the flesh ridden smorgasbord.
Eat up.
Suck slow.
Slow sips.
Slip in.
Out.
Over the hills and thru the wood,
ice skating in the rink;
They call it a Brazilian.
We speak French in our horizontal communications.
We glisten
Sounds of body rain find a melody on our sheets.
Listen-
-as bed legs turn wild horses making leaps.
Squeak, squeak...
Exhausted turns taken in front of bright bathroom sinks.
Time falls into a new digital love,
In the bed, we lay as opposites,
      favorite strangers,
backs turned,
cradling sleep.

Money Shot Ramblings: Somewhere, Near a Window Seat. . .

It doesn't take seeing the movie Jerry McGuire to be familiar with its most popular on-screen line, "show me the money." This phrase captured America's precious heart from the moment it hit the screen and instantly became cemented as part of pop culture. After all, no one wants the money tomorrow. We all want it right now, preferably first! Although in many instances the work is done and the financial reward comes last, we still need some type of assurance that "the money" is coming with certainty. Paperwork such as contracts and promissory notes exist to hold the other party financially responsible, and in the event of a fallout, capable of facing a lawsuit. I believe this is in part due to a lack of trust plus the unforeseeable trait of being taken advantage of.

We all want to either receive our money upfront or know without a doubt that it is coming when it is owed.

Which brings me to Tank. Yes, the R&B singer Tank. One day in late October 2017, he took to Instagram to post a photo from a magazine shoot that I now refer to as his infamous 'money shot.' In it, he was seen gazing out of a picture window while wearing nothing but his boxer briefs. In the comment section, many women wrote about the absence of his penis print. Of course, he also had a legion of supporters, many of which shared the same sentiment of "Maybe he's a grower, not a shower." This got me thinking. My first thought was, "that thang ain't growing into too much more." But I digress.

How much longer are we going to promote the idea of hoping people will grow into what we need vs. accepting what they have shown us. One of Maya Angelou's most cited quotes is probably that of "when people show you who they are, believe them." Why, instead of believing what we've seen, do we think we can wait it out until they grow into what we were hoping for at the three-point line? We can't ask to be shown the money and then refuse to pay attention to the small change that stands in front of us. Women are good for giving men the grower, not a shower safety clause, and exposing ourselves to unnecessary stagnation and disappointment.

This scientific theory may be plausible from the waist down, but from the neck up, it's an insufficient and ill-fated way of forming new relationships. Creating bonds with potential is grounds to get you heartbroken, and when the ship sails, you know who you will be angry at? Yourself!

That dick ain't growing any bigger in 90 more days sis.

Alignment between you and your partner isn't something you should have to grow into. In one relationship, I was told: "to love me and be with me means to accept me where I am and hope I get it together." Listen! A woman should never have to hope one day her man will get on an adult level comparable to hers. A man should be so intent on having himself together that he stays out of the dating game until he can bring more to the table than his bib with a matching knife and fork set and a hard dick that might not be that big!

One of the common denominators in my past relationships has been giving men the space to grow into the person I saw them as having the ability to be. They presented themselves as the Tank picture, and I smiled and told myself, "maybe he's a grower, not a shower." They showed me who they were, and I saw who they could be. At best, growing instead of showing only works in the boxer brief section of the world. But when you consider how small the men's underwear section is in any department store compared to all the other items, that will tell you how important growing a big dick is. A woman would much rather fake orgasms with a small penis attached to a great man than to experience multiple orgasms by a big dick man who is all dick from head to head.

Loving someone's higher self isn't going to translate into them behaving (or loving you) from their higher selves. The result is going to be you, dimming your light and shrinking yourself to fit your love, expectations, and authentic human experience into the tiny pocket on their boxer briefs.

Look at you: Getting caught in a trap. Busting out of the seams. Stressed for easy breathing because it's claustrophobic when you start to reduce yourself and put your needs last.

'Potential' is beautiful. We all have it in some form. But some things can't be compromised into showing me later, and to that point, some people aren't promising to grow later. What you see is what you are going to get most times. If you don't see what you know you need, then the right thing for both parties is to move on. Truth-be-told, everyone is showing their own version of the money shot;

…it's up to you to count the bills and decide if that's ENOUGH.

Let's say you fall in love with a grower (potential), and they don't fall in love with showing (living up to). Congratulations! You've just ended up with the Tank picture, which you can't be too mad at because it's exactly who they **showed** you they were.

Not everyone is going to live up to their potential.

Not every small, flaccid penis is going to turn into a giant, hard dick. Don't settle for growers.

And in the words of the late, legendary Maya Angelou:
"When people show you who they are, believe them."

Yin Yang Ramblings: Somewhere, Waiting on the B Train to Brooklyn...

Love: You don't feel it when it makes its initial contact against your fine body hair, but once it touches down in your aorta, and fills your blood with its adrenaline, and begins to rush through your body...flushing out the negative memories that lay frozen in the forefront of your frontal lobe-
You lose control!
Even after it hurts you...misleads you down false paths, dances and sleeps in front of your mind so you can't see...even after it spits on you, then laughs in your face, Love...never leaves you. It still finds comfort in the silent regions that get the least attention inside of your nervous system. Once it has been developed, it is hardly ever severed from your soul. It can be disconnected from your mind, but in most cases, it lives within your body.

Like: It is the one stand of emotions. It can fuck you dry and still get off. Liking someone doesn't come with the same lifetime warranty. There are no guarantees that person you like today will be the person you like tomorrow. And you don't have to like someone in order to continue to love them. Remember: true Love never dies, but Like does. Like bounces around frivolously; it falls back, falls off and (re)connects with someone else, in another park, sometimes on another ship. "I Like you, I Like you and I Like you, but I LOVE you", is all possible in the mind of Like.

Love is an enigma that gets lost in the folds of our skin while Like dances on top of you, tickling you in places that feel good, which can make you not feel the Love because of the Like and the Like is in your face. Staring in your eyes while Love is napping which would mean you're love blind, so do you even know what's happening???

The yin and the yang.

Imagine sharing your life with someone whom you love but don't like....

Love is the REM sleep while Like is a daydream where you can still see everyone that is passing you.

We give passes and second chances to people because we love them:
>But this sometimes kills how much we like them
>You can love someone and not like them
>You can hurt someone and still love them
>Welcome to relationTRICKS in which true Love never dies but Like does
>So instead of trying to re-bless each other with *"I love you's"* when the status of the emotional esteem
>for one another begins to plummet,
>Why don't we tell the truth;
>The real truth, the whole truth and nothing but the truth.
>Let's be honest with ourselves, our feelings and each other.
>For once while our ships are still sailing along the oceanic waters,
>let's keep it real.
>Ask the question how it should be asked.
>Answer it how it should be answered.
>Not do you still love me, followed by a *'yes I do.'*
>Do you still LIKE ME: *"Yes, I do,"*
>OR
>As a matter a fact, *"No I do not, anymore."*

Chapter Two:
Compromise for What?

.

"Momma don't play chess when the Kings are missing"

AlbuquerQUEEN Ramblings: Somewhere, Near New Mexico, Staring at the Stars...

> *"There is substantial joy in learning how to stop asking Mr. Wrong for the right treatment."*
> *~januarieYork*

You know what? Women sometimes ask Mr. Wrong for all the right stuff. Even after realizing he isn't the right one, we have a nasty habit of thinking we can turn them into Mr. Good Enough. I recently read a comment that said, 'falling in love is a choice.' That's something I didn't believe until recently. But you know what? It IS a choice. We meet, like, and THEN fall in love, but in between the like and the fall, we have intuitions and gut feelings. There are always signs that advise us of what our next move should be (see Money Shot Ramblings p.29). It is our choice on whether we pay attention, and anything that follows is a direct result of that choice. Part of listening to our first instincts begins with our self-love. We cannot adhere to our inner voices if we haven't fallen in love with the woman who bears it. If I don't love myself, why the hell would I trust my gut? And listen, self-love isn't always about how much of it you lack. It's possible to have confidence and know your worth and still need to go the extra mile for yourself. You will know how many more miles you need to travel by the people you choose to share your time with. If you find yourself allowing anyone to reduce you or challenge who you are and what you deserve, you are due to revisit (and possibly upgrade) to your esteem. The keyword there is ALLOW; people will always test you. What we allow is a choice. Discovering your higher-self and embracing loving yourself at that level will change who you choose to allow around you. Stop by a mirror and really take in all that you see. Let go of everything you think you are and rebuild yourself on the spot. If something is missing that you need to confront, do it. Truthfully, it might take the rest of your life. Evolution doesn't end until our energies transcend. But what better way to spend your days than building yourself UP? Control your journey and who is part of it with you.

You are not the passenger, dear heart; you were always the driver!

Make that left turn and find AlbuquerQUEEN.

It's the first left after you finish loving yourself.

Change what you receive forever by how you perceive what you see in the mirror. It will favorably influence how you love and who you allow to love you back.

Compromise for What?

Skeletons

I'm trying to unpack your baggage and mine.
You're behind me
trying to slam the luggage down on my hands.
I'm in front of you with a box of my confessions,
and a bag of your past. You're not in the
right position sir!! This is the point where I grab my bags and
walk out the door, never to return.
If we stop the fight right here, no one will get dirty.
But if we continue
like this
With me as the baggage concierge holding your
elephant man bones, and you
as a customer to be served who can do no wrong.
I'll need a walk-in closet to hold the skeletons
you will have left on
and with me.

Crash

Intertwined like mangled steel wrapped around utility poles.
Wounded bleeding holes
in hearts
get bandaged with the airbags of another's protection.
We've crashed into each other.
Erections are hardening.
Panties are moistening.
Hearts are healing.
Blood is racing.
Clocks are ticking.
Ships are sinking.
Emotions are speeding.
Head on collisions are inevitable and before we all know:
We crash.

Compromise

Who did you fall in love with,
if not the person
you are presently seeking to change?

Look In Fly

I looked good on his arm
as if I were candy paint decorating his suit jacket;
cherry red on suicide doors.
My sepia arm dripping in jewels like daytime glitter.
Alternating from faux to French diamonds,
because every girl needs costume jewels.
Accessorizing his east side accent
like English language
blanketing German subtitles.
The paparazzi loved the way we made an entry.
Arms crisscrossing melanins,
Brown skin blending,
We looked fly together
But I was interlocking elbows
with an anchor that could halt the Titanic.
My born wings at ease for my soldier,
"known to carry big things if you know what I mean"
…like a lofty conceit
and an enormous ego with substantial needs
famous for drowning my plans and birthing new anxieties.
I watched him clip and collect my feathers in his back pocket
We wouldn't want my ascent to emasculate his stand still
He was my weight
Holding me at bay, changing my view of myself,
Crystallizing my confidence in concrete suffocation

Pulling me towards the no-fly list in between
selfies that generated
hundreds of likes.
My smile was coated in bride to be
heart stuffed with olive tasting Hope,
Green with mold it incurred from waiting to exhale,
Looking back on this ex hell, I see hindsight through the Lasik
surgery of my soul windows
We looked fly together but in between takes
We were hungry for what we each really wanted.
So, my IG feed became my protein while
I was grounded in disembarkment
from the pressure his downward pulling muscles
placed on my free flying left arm,
interwoven inside the handcuff of his right
making him glow
feeding his ego a seven course meal
While myself,
starving for the flight
my incarcerated wings were created for.
…and when I let go of his knotless tie,
Beyond the scope of my own control,
I began again
To …

Love Ramblings: Somewhere, at a Rest Stop Near Vegas...

Love is a great fucking feeling, right? I mean, even if you don't know what it feels like to be loved properly, the fantasies you have created about it are still so extraordinary that the expectation is that of potential splendor. Once love has been established in relationships, I admit some of us women go completely off the deep end. We give all that we have, including but not limited to our bodies, soul (ties), calendars, benefits of the doubt, and of course, the most valuable of all: our time. The person who is being loved is receiving the harvest of their lover. Ideally and through healthy reciprocity, both parties are playing two parts: the lover and the loved.

But as we all know, many times in a two-person relationship, one person is doing all the receiving without returning the **act** of love. It feels good to know that you have someone you can depend on, even if you have no intention of being that person for them. That ego stroke tastes like an afternoon glass of a 30-year-old Scotch, being sipped on the balcony of a Portofino cliffside manor. But it's an unfair means of relating. Who is refilling the person that is doing all the pouring? You can only do so much pouring out before you are empty within, and then what?

We get so heart-bent on keeping the man we love that we buy into this faux-fantasy that suggests you can love a man into loving you. Admittedly, I've tried it myself, so I speak from experience when I say all you'll end up doing is yelling for help out of the labyrinth of mind fucks. Take note of two things:

1. A man will not STOP you from loving him, and

2. You deserve more than "I love you."

On an episode of BET's "Being Mary Jane," during a confrontation between Mary Jane and her ex, she passionately yelled about having been a "ride or die" chick for him. As she listed the many ways she had accommodated his every need, a prolific exchange happened that reigns true in real life, not just the reel one.

David: "I never asked you to do any of that."
MJ: "You never told me to stop either!"
David: Why would I stop a woman from loving me?"

It was at that point that I was introduced to my exes.

You should know that many men will NOT stop you from loving them. If the benefits are stellar, he's not going to want to cut that rope as it's useful to him. He'll continue to let you pamper him in whatever you provide to him (sex, money, time, affection, etc.), even when he knows he shouldn't. It's hard to stop someone from making you feel good. We are all guilty. It's not a man or a race thing. It's human nature to want to feel good and receive more of it, even when we are still searching for the missing key.

But you deserve better than that.

The words 'I love you' are a cute mouth accessory and when they somersault from lips that you frequently kiss, you hope they are believable. The ears may be pleased by what they hear, but a shallow I love you unsupported by action, respect of love languages and eagerness to learn and grow together, are just three useless words. Love is an experience. If there is no true soul-binding connection being shared, all you will ever feel is what it's like to be pierced all over by letters that gathered to form a lie. Ok, not everyone is lying. Some folks just cannot love you the way you need to be loved, and that's fine, but um…MOVE OUT THE WAY THEN!

You deserve more than sentiments shared with absent actions.

You deserve more than a metaphoric collision of ears and hope.

If his interest in you doesn't turn a corner that is too high for his dick to reach, the only conscious act he will do with you is reap the benefits of you loving him. Your love for him will not turn his heart dial to face you. It will not prevent him from leaving, cheating, dry-begging, and using or hurting you. Loving someone who doesn't or can't love you back is an independent act of which you will receive no medal or praise.

You deserve more than an I love you from a man who will not stop you from loving him.

Lack of reciprocity will create a monster in dying need of affection. Continuing in a situation where you aren't emotionally fed can leave a devastating aftertaste on your tongue. If you choose to carry on through your imaginary field of flowers, know that you are simply pacifying his needs; you are not creating a love story. He, on the other hand, will continue allowing himself to be covered in your affection good deeds. And can you blame him?

Love is not as difficult as we make it. It should be stable and grounded in understanding. Love shouldn't feel like the death of you, nor should it make you feel bad about yourself or your decisions. Stop accepting I love you's from the caves of fool's gold mines, tucked behind break-heart mountains. Tame your heart and start listening to your inner-goddess; she's looking out for you (see Finding AlbuquerQUEEN Ramblings p.36). You were born as love; therefore, anyone giving you a lesser version of yourself is already striking out.

Nina Simone said it best: "We have to learn to leave the table when love is no longer being served." You deserve not to be served food on trash can lids or to be eating air on porcelain plates. Love is an action verb. Those three words should only be a verbal reminder of the constant and consistent energy being served.

You deserve MORE –
– WAY more –
than JUST an I Love You for your ear.

You deserve to BE LOVED, so righteously, that your soul FEELS it forever.

DNR Order

Authenticity is as necessary as fresh air to breathe in.

Characters can only live

through the psyche of the architect.

There is no totem in real life,

You are

who you are.

Inception:

There are no alternative endings.

Compromise for What?

PenmanShit

As soon as my ink touches them
They are dead.
They become
mink stoles in the middle of country roads
killed
by tires rotating at sixty miles per hour.
As soon as my ink touches them,
they lose power and light.
They obliterate and leave not even a trace of blood spatter.
Nothing exists
but the repetition of my memories and the failure of
my discernment:
I know better.
I'm not supposed to let my ink touch the drink.
It's poison to man-veins.
My writings are dripped in pain like
white diamonds and pearl linens,
finer things,
pinky finger extended,
hand fans waving hellos from behind the shade.
My writings are liquid gunshots
melting over the heart and breaking
the cease fire.
I retired my desire for penning poems
to unsung songs between me
and the man that fit the title of my king
because every time I do,

when I Pen Man Shit,
my penmanship makes me a murderer.
My rhyming lines and heavily described sentences
ends with nine lives
draped over broken picket fences with not even
one heartbeat between them all.
I bleed my relationships dry for poetry,
slowly leaking details
of every stage
in saved documents for later stages.
Literal death. Literary crime.
Next time I fall for the edges
where love meets the creases of my eyes,
I won't scribe anything.
...but what if that's not what changes the outcome?

Compromise for What?

Live from the Comedy Theater

You think I'm a joke;
I think you are laughable.
This does not mean we are compatible in the slightest.

Destruction I

Some men want to steal from you,
in broad daylight,
they will break in making no noise.
Jump fences
hop roofs and crack open unlocked windows to
destroy you.
Silently they prey on you
with hands touching hands touching a
supposed God that they couldn't possibly believe in.
They will try to murder your belief
Jump it in the street,
leave it chalk lined for a law & order scene,
cut to the chase of things.
No time to waste on rings
when lies can be outfitted to wrap around
left fingers that still stand tall,
break her so she won't leave you.
Make her feel small and disjointed
Lacking the beauty she possessed
when you first met,
make her a conquest
beat your chest
bark across the street
holler at the moon
kiss the girls and make them lie down with you
so you can stroke her into cardiac detest

Compromise for What?

Lauryn said, "Girl, you know you better watch out!"
The easiest way to control is by removing all confidence.
If he can make you think he's the best,
even while giving only his worst
while constantly highlighting your worst,
got you inhaling your flaws for brunch,
then he will become the supervisor
and he will remain out to lunch on you
and you will wither away from a thirst that keeps you
dehydrated,
and unfulfilled by his kisses
though you will use them
as your water
and you will drink
until you are emotionally slaughtered.
And it will taste like cyanide.
Pay attention when something tastes bitter and burns your tongue

Richard

Big dick

Hard dick

Hand on dick

Ready to stick

Twenty four seven shift

Shit

Dick get sick when balls are blue

Dick get mad when words aren't true

When bust ain't open

And lips ain't smoking the suck out of its peace pipe

Piece of pipe

Dick pie

Dickmitized

Black man, don't be stigmatized

By what's hanging in between your thighs

Thick size

Widened eyes for soul ties

Dick gon' cry when it ain't stroking the prize

Big dick

Hard dick

Dick in hand

Dick got plans to land

Inland

As much as it can

Dick get mad if you fall asleep

Dick sending texts for the TLC "Creep"

Compromise for What?

Be careful who you meet
Cause Dick gonna keep
Itself happy
But STD's
are happening
at an alarming rate
and side-chick periods have no problems being late.
Dick needs to get a check up
Dick needs to lift his neck up
Cause there's a head up-
Top. Dick needs to stop being so entranced by itself
It's good health to love the higher self a little bit more
Unlimited body count makes you
look like a whore. *No woman wants to wife a dickwhore.
Dick needs to let Richard call the shots a lil' more
Let the man have the floor
Open up and show your core
You'll never fuck away your pain. It's a shame, did no one
ever call you by your first name, Richard?
Stop being led by your dick
Big dick. Calling the shots.
Hard dick. Thick and hot.
Dick in hand. Feeling all grand.
But dick ain't worth a damn if it ain't attached to a good man.

He's feeding me castor oil.
Telling me it will ease the butterflies in my stomach but-

What's going to ease the buzzing of my intuition???

Cryola

Candy colored promises

broken like crayon pieces,

lining up the halls and walls

of the home that became our dwelling of emotional mayhem.

Sugar Daddy

I redefined daddy as a sexual colloquialism
to be used only over the brown shoulders
of a man whose penis size
was big enough to make me do more
than
...wince.
Or fake.
I've always felt protection during sex
Despite the fact that
protection is something I've had to beg and
convince men to indulge in.
I'm a clean looking gal I suppose.
...and strong enough for single motherhood,
should that cum.
Their arms tighten around my body,
drawing me closer to the inner workings
of their increasing heartbeat,
kissing me like my whole body is my forehead.
It all feels soft and at home.
They hold hands with me as if our bodies becoming one
was us crossing a busy street.
"Daddy," I whisper with a moan to follow.
Their ego swells through the head of our connecting cable
and from point of entry through completion,
they become a new definition of daddy:
Someone who's right in front of me
yet still somehow missed.
Giving sugar in exchange for unspoken long
goodbyes and missed hugs.
I once wrote
"Some men are looking for a daughter to fuck"
...and now I know
some women are looking for a daddy
to love.

Destruction II

Or have you not yet learned it....

.... are you still learning?

That your love

is too plentiful to turn down,
...too gigantic to sew up,
and too fancy
to let grow?

...Test Dummies

We crash
Selfishly avoiding our pain
with the lack of procrastination to push
the petal to the metal and cruise for brighter skies
Automatically shifting from the neutral space
of once warm beds
now cold with animosity,
and drive down the secret lover's lane of lies
Wondering if the other side really has greener grass,
yet prepared for a rendezvous that won't last
past the next set of footprints the sun
leaves across the sky.
We've each unlocked our seatbelt
And are being thrust towards windshields
that will eventually cave
outwards as the bodies of love,
infatuation and desire fly out
...and we will lie on the ground
...no one next to each other...
Separate...
But equal
Band-Aids' can't heal our scars,
now permanent.
And we will sit amongst each other,
Together, yet still alone
Intertwined like mangled steel wrapped around utility poles

Mars and Venus,

now worlds apart,

yet growing closer together

We drive

We speed

We prepare

To crash

Only to discover

We should have just stayed home

All these dicks,
And not a healthy Richard in sight.

Tragedy.

Eight Hundred Two Seven Three, Eight Two Five Five

I found the number
to the suicide hotline
on the back patio where I decided to sleep.
She spoke to me in a soft tone.
Drifted with me out to the ocean of tears and
pulled me back with the tides of her soothing
words of comfort. She was my rose bush
at 2 in the morning.
He slept soundly.
Upstairs.
Giving his snores the right to converse with
the silence of our home.
The argument was over.
But the impact was stinging me in my ribs.
It burned my throat when I swallowed my truth.
Who am I if not capable of love?
How does one who makes love feel above the earth
make hurt feel beneath soil
while burying me
in the rigor mortis of harsh words?
Does he even make love feel above the earth?
Suddenly, I had new questions.
I asked her to talk me off the ledge
that I knew I didn't belong
on.
I could see her fear from the screen of my cell phone,

She knew

Like I knew

That the one thing I needed to keep me alive,

was to kill the relations

between he and I,

and set this ship free with the tide

Compromise for What?

Chapter Three:
The Edge of the Cliff

"I'd have moved every letter in the alphabet for you"

Scattered Brain

I'm on the floor full of poems
sorting through words I've stifled
and thoughts I interrupted
in an effort to love
unconditionally.

A Familiar Name (For Colored Girls, 2014)

I believe that bruises
that are gifted by hands
that once held the expectation of protection
hurt a little more than those
that come from strangers.
At least strangers never promised you with serenading eyes.
Strangers never gave birth to levees,
now broken,
no longer holding back the water
that falls from lips
busted during violent thrusting in
and out,
this space,
that once held fairytale like possibilities,
now eclipsed into permanent
midnight hour.
Strangers don't hold hands with honor,
only to squander away its possibilities
because the ego has a need to be fulfilled
by fear.
Strangers don't earn your confidence,
and boogie men don't step out
looking like boogie men in the light.
It would have cut less into the heat of my life
if the thief that stole
my right to be woman
were unknown to me like an unopened bill.

Instead, he wore a sophisticated coat
and an expensive smell
And a smile that I invited into the center
of my comfort zone
An exquisite face, and a familiar name
A name I saved and called and contacted using MY voice
A name that leapt from my lips like unicorns,
dashing through valleys
of musical pearl roses
I sang his name in four-part harmonies,
I let him know me!
Did he see inside of my head whispers
and decide to punish me for
daring to be Jezebel with the way I held his hand
It's like my chromosome was his public enemy
He approached me seductively
with no knives to my back
and no guns to my side
This non-stranger with a familiar name
bore arms full of my trust
and reassurance
And used them as duct tape across my lips.
I blessed him with my time
Gifted him my benefit of the doubt
I gave him the right to see me dance with high twirls
of lifted cheekbones
Smiling all up his beautiful!
Sacrificial dear diary entries falling in his lap

My gospel truth stolen
The youth taken from my step
My dreams now sloppy,
sleeping with fingers on switchblade
handles and gripping the panic button when I sleep
This is a nightmare for colored girl sheets,
devoured, manipulated
and treated to slave regimen
by a man who was an encouraged
visitor-
-but not a proposed alien-like transient
who hopped out of the alley
while I was carrying my groceries
He was his own intentional intruder
And the only mask he wore
was the one that never showed across
his face
His hands were not beastly
Eyes were not red
There were no horns coming out of his head
Only inner demons fighting away my power
He wore a grey suit
And gave me flowers
And his coat when I got cold
And he walked me home in the rain.
He gave me reason to believe in a nonstranger
with a familiar name.

The Edge of the Cliff

Surgery Ramblings: Somewhere, Near the Atlantic Ocean

Here's some permission you never needed:

Find you. Love you. Choose you.

Choosing ourselves over the nouns that come into our lives and compromise who we are is one of the most significant steps in the direction of a thriving human experience. Selfishness is a form of self-care that you will need to rely on more than a few times. You won't be able to thrive while participating in relationships that leave you feeling left out or like a supporting cast member. It may even hurt to choose you sometimes; it can be like a surgery with no anesthesia. Something will be removed or taken out, and you will be forced to move on without it. But you'll still have yourself, which you'll lose if you stick around in unhealthy situations.

Welcome to the Intensive Care Unit. Proceed with caution and extreme care. Look around you as there are questions you will need to ask to be released from this floor. When you are searching for the answers, be sure to open discernment's door for the people, places and/or things that you need to let go of. In one of the earlier seasons of Grey's Anatomy, Dr. Christina Yang was treating a trauma patient and had to ask him three crucial questions before she could move forward with treatment. Those questions, "Do you know who you are," "do you know what happened to you," and "do you want to live this way" are the questions you will need to ask yourself to complete this surgery.

Do you know who you are − − *What are your perceptions of the world and of life? What brings you joy, and what causes you grief or pain? What upsets you? How do you love? Are you awake, alert, and involved, or are you just existing? What do you want for yourself? What would make you feel successful? What are your dreams, and what have you done to achieve or dismiss them?*

Do you know what has happened to you —*What caused you to think and feel the way you do? Are you ok with that? Who hurt you? Who made you laugh? Where were you when the ball dropped? What did it look like when you got back up? How long were you down? Are you ready for a return to flying? What has caused you to fear, and what has helped you believe? Who did or do you run to? Did you know that you own the rights to everything that has happened to you? Now, what are you going to do with that?*

Do you want to live this way – *How can this answer be YES?! If you died today, on a scale of one to five with five being the highest possible feeling, how would you rate your overall satisfaction with how you lived your life? What surgery needs to be done to achieve a five, and can you start today? Scalpel anyone?*

Kintsugi

I am not broken

or disrupted

I am not battered

or rendered useless

I am everything I've spoken over years

I am every flight that I flew

thru tears

I am not a hoe. I am not my ass.

I am bigger than an orgasm that only lasts for seconds.

…*orgasms only last for seconds.* I'm bigger than

that. I am a gift

a blessing

I am a conduit

anything but less

more than just sex.

Not to be reduced

lost

I am pissed

But I am a restoration on God's next up list.

I am anything

but broken.

Missou

Listening to the dark
while tasting the scent of what missing you
feels like.
Sensory Observation.

Edge of the Cliff

You seem like easy sailing and good times.
But I can only offer you my hand,
and you can brush past it ever so gently while holding open the door.
I make no promises
or guarantees. I wear anxiety
as a sweater
for the winter days and a
scarf for cool spring evenings.
I'm safely wrapped in my noticeable standoffishness,
and I'd be lying if I said I don't like how it feels; it fits me.
I'm in stage three of dopamine addiction recovery and probably
overprotective of me.
I do not seek to love you.
Or trust you past the proven moment.
I will not give you much of me;
only surface dust and characteristics too big to hide.
I wear fear as my pride and I am I proud to be
Scared . . . guarded,
perfectly lonely and safe.
And emotionally free.

3 AM Musing

I wanna watch TV
I wanna turn it off
I'm hot, then I'm too cool.
Close the window,
Open the curtain
I'm wide awake
And sleepy
Tired.
I wanna turn on the TV
I wanna smoke.
Or have an orgasm.
Or go to sleep
Maybe write a poem, and
Get on Facebook.
#Scroll
I should turn off the TV
Save energy
Go to sleep
Work is in less than three hours
I should close my eyes
But my mind is being showered with thoughts.
I wanna watch TV
Lay on my side
Wait-
I'm wiSe awake.
Wide at stake

Brain wants to think
And check Facebook
#Scroll
Go to IG
Post three pics
One more
Remove all four before dawn.
Sleepy me,
Wanting to watch TV
Or smoke
Or blog
Write a poem perhaps?
Is that my stomach growling?
Or the phone ringing in my head?
I should sit up
It's hot
I'm sweaty
The dogs are sleep
I wanna watch TV
I wanna go to bed.
3 AM Musings.
I want to go to sleep
And forget that you're no longer there.

Strength Ramblings: Somewhere, Near the Pacific Coast Highway

My grandmother was a woman of much strength. I was about 36 years old when I saw her crying for the first and only time. It was so startling to me that I didn't even know how to process what I saw and attributed her tears to excessive yawning. All I knew was Netria Parker Marlin only showed two emotions — anger and joy. In that moment, we were sharing a different experience. My grandmother gave no breath to feelings of melancholy or anything likewise. As a matter of fact, she denounced heartache and frowned upon unnecessary whining and crying. As it was told to me, she had been that way since she was a child. After she passed from Alzheimer's in 2017, I spent a lot of time remembering that day, I saw her crying. I wondered how many bottled up emotions were present in her face full of tears. I've also had curiosities regarding the effects of bottled up emotions and how that might relate to developing Alzheimer's disease. Still, I have yet to research the scientific correlation.

Throughout our brutal American history, black women were beaten and brutalized for showing their despair and affections. Our elders learned that, at times, their survival would depend on their ability to remain psychologically reserved no matter what was happening. They were expected to be restrained and quiet; black courage could cost black lives, babies, and children included. Resultingly, our ancestral women began practicing a casual, disconnected approach. Those who mastered hiding their anguish and their revelry became the prototype black girls were advised to reference throughout development. We are taught that strong women don't cry. Instead, they thrive and survive with a stoic, unmovable disposition that isn't quickly troubled or shaken by life's occurrences.

Strength became synonymous with emotional detachment. It was the main characteristic of the women who appeared to keep it all together. Those whose despair didn't disturb her facial expressions and whose bruises created no commotion (much like my grandmother). There's a virtue of tenacity displayed in the ability to control one's feelings. But I've learned that strength is not one dimensional and exuding too much of it can have devastating psychological effects.

On any given day, our emotions might be pulled in several directions at once, with each asking for our attention. I believe that ignoring or not confronting what you genuinely feel about something or someone is a weakening agent. It backs up in your solar plexus, lessening your self-control and internal power, running you the risk of spontaneous combustion. Now, there is an art to confronting your emotions that I don't think can be dictated, only guided by the advice of others. You must know what's best for you and how to properly speak your mind. Giving yourself permission to experience your personal human journey authentically is step one in strength-building exercises.

Allowing your considerations room to breathe doesn't make you an emotional, unstable creature like my grandmother may have thought. It teaches you how to navigate what you feel, when to be silent, and when to speak up because while silence can be healthy, it can always be a way to elevate the enemy. The right silence at the wrong time can earn muscles for swine seeking to feed off passivity. My therapist would say, "Walk in your truth." Allow yourself to experience sorrow as much as joy, pains with pleasures, and your lows with your highs. Grieve. Shout. Cry. Be angry and charged. Don't linger and dwell in sadness, but you should waltz on a private dancefloor with your innermost thoughts. It's the only way of healing and preventing future emotional suffering while exercising the sincerest form of strength. You can't conquer the bench press if you refuse to acknowledge that some weights need lifting. The day I saw my grandmother crying, I believe it was for everything she had never shed a tear for.

Don't be so strong that you forget to feel, and sis,

Do not kill yourself with strength.

Junkie Shyt

The veins in my arm are broken
battered and bruised
So, I invite you over
and place my feet on you

I gotta get high somehow.

7 A.M.

I slept in my clothes last night
A dress
u liked.
Tried to lure u into my dream.
I needed to sleep with u.
Next to u.
Yearned in my turning for your affectionate snores.
A touch of my hand to your shoulder blade.
A glimpse into your sleep when my head is on your pillow,
I needed u
to fall asleep.
So I slept in my clothes
A dress.
One u liked to see
me in.

I waited for u
At the embankment of inception.
Kicking feet.
Dangling legs.
Flower dress.
I checked my watch.
It was fifteen past the hour when your car pulled up.
Suicide doors opened with so much at stake.
My cell fell out of my purse as I stood.
Reality check: alarm clock was ringing.
Time to wake,
still in that dress you liked to see me in.

Ghost Zaddy

Tell your ghost to stop leaving your scent on my pillow,
and I will tell my human self
to stop
resurrecting you in my bed.

Stuff

Matter

Material

Articles

Activities

Specified

Indeterminate

Referenced.

Stuff…. immortalized in definition

But when it comes to our —

Intuition

Stuff matters more

We see stuff.

We know it.

Ignore stuff.

Overlook it like we don't care.

Loving wildly and vividly with our palms wide open

Fast receivers.

Fingers caressing the outside temperature,

Four hundred internal degrees of pre-made vows

Waiting for the right turn,

Left hand

Diamonds against the melanin

We don't back down

Thrusting towards the future with our Ray-Bans testing the sunlight

Against the grain of the stuff we see.

We travel

With the speed of a fighter's right hook

And along the way

She cries again

Our intuition

In need of attention and a bit of

Listening.

She makes our stomach growl

Though we are not hungry

Our menstruals

Become messier

Longer

More unpredictable…like twice a month.

We have less patience.

And zero tolerance.

The noise of love making drowns out the sound of our

inner voice

with dopamine

and stuff gets overlooked

Emotional stuff

Stuffed in glad bags with no twisty ties,

Wide open stuff.

Sexual stuff.

Shrouded and hidden.

Uncovered in lies that smell like a few too many spins of Tupac.

All eyes on the stuff we ignore.

We try to live with it.

We don't believe it

As a matter a fact,
We retrieve it
From the doorsteps
Back porches
Front yards
Walk in closets
Pants and jacket pockets
and don't forget the leather wallets
of the ones we think we were selected to save,
and 'bring the good out' of.
Stuff….
We take it all
Push it into our bosom until it turns into electricity in our heart
This is how a screwed beat starts.
We pack it in our suitcases,
Hiding our own personal findings
We take stuff
We take their stuff
Also known as shit
And treat it like mulch to our bed of seeds,
Laying in it, awaiting the arrival of flower we already are.
But spring only comes once a year and too damned often,
after coloring across the lines of the page,
and evading our ESP,
We realize there is too much shit in this bed.
This is only a Queen
And there is but one choice.

Either this stuff will produce the birth of new blooms,
Or
this yard
My yard,
will burst with blossoms
Minus all this -
All His,
Unacknowledged
Avoided
Harmful and dangerous
Stuff._
I choose the latter.

Chapter Four:
The eXquisite Pain, 3463

What I want is an Earth shattering,
tailspin of two worlds colliding above the
bed that galaxies make. I want to listen to the storms
roll off his tongue and I will eat them until we tornado back into
the sunlight. Horizons rising to the zen of our hocus pocus. A love that could
build a new Eiffel Tower, a journey that feels like every step is paradise.
A place where I see the truth and receive an endless,
fruitful supply of conditional, unconditional love.
Because let's be honest,

...all love has conditions.

EL oh EL

I guess....
I could fly....
off and above, soaring higher than your memories
dancing harder than your feet would allow,
I guess I always was
...a solo lip sync.
I guess I could find my space
my place in God's arms for real, for real,
I could
I guess
locate where I want to live
be
where there is warmth
and stars are shooting by
and if I'm lucky, maybe even an ocean breeze
I guess I could find me
again.
I guess maybe this time I never lost her
and that was my biggest flaw for you
I can't lose me
to fit you
because life has shown me that every time I do that,
I lose.
Everything.
I guess I could write poems again
and blog my pain
without repercussion or rush to unnecessary judgment,
I guess I could breathe
take pics in the Bahamas for the world to see
I guess I could go somewhere and live
and do what I love to do most: Just Be.
Or....
I could forego all of that new growth
and stay with you.
Laughing out loud
Literally.

Word Ramblings: Somewhere, Traveling by Train...

If you love freely and soulfully enough, you won't want to pierce your companion with words. You will protect them, even from your own anger. You will pause, before you speak because:

Words hurt.
...and linger,

And words...are CHOSEN.

(T)HugzMansion

There are echoes in my home
A hallway of ghosts
and tumbleweeds
with heart shards as wall border.
This California King
was bigger than the crown
you fumbled to want to wear.

So, I took down your pictures
with a smile, and called your name from downstairs
expecting only the loudest to hug my ears in response
I stuffed our love story behind the brick walls in the basement
A time capsule for the next tenant to tour.

I spend my days unpacking
and nights laughing
and my voice bounces off the walls of this space I nicknamed
"(t)Hugz Mansion"
Echoes bubbling over like high heat pasta water
I don't regret letting go
I only wish
I had done it much sooner.

Check Ya'self Que(EN)

This is not *just* my voice.

This -

is a roll call

and a head count.

To all the spirits tired of loving in the wrong directions

Those who are done soul sharing without protection,

This is the call to our recklessness;

Check ya'self Que-

Care more about your life, your health

...and maybe even your next breath!

This is the sound of a mirror talk with self-

> **Where are you at QueEN???**
> **Please adjust your crown!!!**

This is the ear-piercing music notes to our exposé

We so often write our own pain and then live in

between the lines we made, yet we blame the characters we created.

Monsters and Frankenstein's whose seeds were sown

in our basements.

Stop wasting precious time I say to myself.

Pick up your mat and walk the bible says to me!

Clarity is yours, Godspeed,

What else do you need but *faith* that whatever it is trying to break

you down can be superseded with the right amount of brave?

This is a call to be your own hero so that you can

face whatever is next. For as long as there is a next breath-

there will always be a new test.

We are tasked with being honest with ourselves.
Stepping off the pawn block and getting back to our square.
There's an "EN" stomping at the end of our "QUE!"
Dare to Check Ya'self Que!
So stop biting off more than you can chew and
quit trying to break down gristle with your teeth.
May this inspire women everywhere to stay on beat.
No more tears for the wrong woman's son.
No more strapping the wrong ideas onto reality's hoist.
This is the beat of broken silence
This is the crack of a life-changing choice
The authorization for personal accountability.
*This is anything but **just** my voice.*

Stuff II

All this stuff
Pardoned
Forgiven without explanation; *without conversation.*
Stuff.
Excused and condoned
at the expense of our garden.
Stuff
We see it
We ignore it
We go forward anyway,
Pushing past the barriers and barreling into love
Head first like a raging bull
Everything is red and beautiful
Like valentines
But hearts aren't indestructible
And the St. was a maniac.

Stuff doesn't stop us.
But it should.
It really should…
Some stuff
Should really make us
Stop.

Jill Ramblings: Somewhere, Near the Smoky Mountains

Rest Stop Thoughts: "Look at you, nigga. I would've taken your secrets to the grave, but you out here banking on a Pasty Patsy to be your entrusted confidante. Is she a better listener than I? Or was it purely sexual? Did she taste like the whole milk or skim I see when I look at her? When black men were being killed back to back by police, all in a week, did she provide you proper comfort? I giggle in sarcasm at the idea that she might be better equipped to handle the perils of black life better than me or that her worth was of greater value than mine. That's my interpretation of it. You're suggesting to me, no matter how unintentional, that this white woman was worth risking everything we shared. That our black love paled in comparison to the soul ties you willingly shared with her. And now look: she turned on you and sold you out for sport, yet, you put more trust in her than me. Poetic justice, I tell ya! Let me reread what she sent me again..."

It's been said that [sometimes] black men turn to white women because they are more docile and drama-free; they know their places. I've heard that last line numerous times. They don't use sex as a bargaining chip and are eager to please their king no matter what it takes. I'm not saying these things are true or representative of all white women. I'm simply repeating some of the bullshit hearsay I've collected over the years. For the record, wanting to please your man and not treating intercourse like a weapon aren't bad characteristics, nor are they characteristics reserved solely for white women. But they are used as pedestal pushers against black women. The black women who are mouthier and stand up for themselves without pause often find themselves at the tail end of this comparison. This reminds me of the cliché 'angry black woman.' This disparaging remark is used against any black woman who isn't exercising her right to remain silent in most situations. The woman who finds this label attached to her collarbone will most likely be compared to the silence of white women.

Despite my personal experiences, I still believe in the possibility of monogamy. I believe it to be a personal, psychological choice that must be powerful enough to override all outside physical influence. But I also know the inventory of those who do cheat, sometimes repeatedly, is vast and fully stocked. Because of this, I believe plenty of women are prepared to deal with cheating IF that person is the one she deems worthy of such a grand fight to regain trust. I am in no way condoning cheating. I call bullshit on the inability to control yourself from sharing intimacy (in its variety of forms) with someone outside of your person. I'm also not convinced that forgiveness equates to it never occurring again. If you don't possess enough mind control to refrain from becoming involved with someone outside of your companion, then you need to be single. Or communicate your polyamorous desires in the beginning. Allow people to make choices for themselves instead of being damaged by betrayal. Don't be out here handing out unhealthy, tapas-style love and calling it a safe relationship. STAY SINGLE.

Quick question though: was cheating a total deal-breaker ever? Seriously, let's think about it. Do we believe that folks who made it to Gold and Silver anniversaries got there without drama? Tuh! Most folks can't even cross the fifth year without knocking someone else down (or up). So, it's possible for cheating to not be the end-all of a relationship, although it will be the beginning of a long, complicated, almost nomadic journey back to each other. But if cheating is something my black man feels he needs to do, and I'll speak solely for myself on this, let the other woman be Black.

There is no denying that all betrayal, in this case, cheating, is hurtful. Cheating produces doubt and questions where there may have otherwise been confidence and belief. Beyond the standard negative outcomes of cheating, interracial affairs create a further complication: the invisibility of the black woman in a relationship that she thought was sacred. It's been happening since the beginning of our time here. The erasure of black women feels like an open-to-the-public, interactive art exhibit of which all are encouraged to participate (including other black people). Not only can this be emotionally traumatic, but it can have you feeling like the world is watching and collectively, not giving a fuck.

America continues to attempt to devalue and dismiss the

importance, beauty, and necessity of black women in this world. Our movements are hijacked without initial credit to us. See #MeToo. We are the lowest paid in the workforce despite our increasingly rising education stats. And in the movies, our representation is too often predictably centered on sex, slavery, or angry and single. It's rather cumbersome, so when a black man cheats on us with a white woman, it feels like a two-sided, jagged edge, hot blade branding new anger on our heart valves. The sting is different when it's a white woman on the writing side of Shirley Murdock's hit song, "As We Lay."

Of course, this could just be my story.

Or, it might be that black women are simply fucking tired of being erased. It happens everywhere from publishing and media to corporate America, so when our personal spaces and relationships are violated, we might be low on understanding. I know I was. White women have been the belle of the United States ball since its inception. They have inadvertently defined for our society what it means to be a mother, a wife, and a woman. The white woman is America's Crown and Glory, while the black woman epitomizes its dark shadows and secrets. We're seen as loud and untamed, wild, and fluorescent. America loves pastel. White women are pastels.

You know what the biggest gripe about cheating is? It makes the other person feel insufficient. At the center of it all, the biggest sore spot is the one where you begin to question yourself, especially if you have been blindsided. No matter the selfish intention, being cheated on says, 'you were not good enough, and this person was better.' The action verb of what this new person is 'better' at can be anything: listening, having sex, laughing, talking, etc. . . . The bottom line is it feels like they scored higher on the SATs while you sit with a broken pencil, still trying to solve question three on your fingers. When you add race into the equation, it becomes a special sort of trauma. Not only are you saying I do not satisfy you enough, but to add insult to injury, this white woman is better than me?

This white woman
is better
at loving a black man,
my black man,
than me?
Interesting concept.

Black women need sacred spaces where we can light up the room as our natural selves. It should be a place of peace and love where we don't have to put up a fight or throw on our favorite Superwoman capes to live under the "twice as hard" theory. We need to be able to let our guard down too. I know it's hard out here for black men, but who gave birth to them and what makes them think our roads are paved in pillow tops? Our personal companion-relationships (when applicable) should be one of those sacred places where trust, respect, and love are in abundant supply. If unhappiness exists in a way that conversation and subsequent actions don't correct, then the loving, respectful, black-lives-matter thing to do is to part ways.

Black women shouldn't have to fight to be number one to a white woman anywhere…

…but especially at home in our own fucking beds.

Eugene Street

I'm done here.
No more of this-
Rummage sale reject,
thrift store shopping
Free shipping,
Back alley handling,
      -or mishandling
$5 DVD bin,
No movies I want in this muthaf%&@~
Half off, dollar store,
Section wait --- hate value,
Boxed up,
Laboratory trash
Petri dish leftovers
mop water tasting, time wasting
Bullshit chasing,
Re-Dick-U-Lust,
Unrequited,
Complete fallacy of the truth,
Ex-factor,
No tax,
No retractor,
Charitable donation,
Write off,
Rap off,
Off rap,
Pink cookies in a plastic bag
getting crushed by
feelings
type of love.

This class is permanently dismissed.

eXquise, mi Amor

iF you aren't the worth
tHe golden tickets
tHe coupon to come back for more
iF you aren't the tap of the golden cymbal,
oR the love of snare
iF you aren't the spin
tHe turn
tHe burning of the midnight oil at 3 o'clock in the morning
iF you aren't a salacious sub-stat
a post
aN insomniac's host of sheep counts
iF that horse isn't mounted
rEady for gallops away
iF you aren't the messiah to my runaway aortic valves
iF
yOu aren't the vow of kitchenette kisses
tHe veil of truth
iF you aren't the intention I lie under
oR the youthful smile that never ceases to take me
aSunder
sHit
-mAke me wonder-
iF you aren't the receiver
oF a free write
iN a social media stat
dUring daylight working hours
iF the powers that be
dId not make you the reason i see highlights while
dRiving
oR the chest that I love nose diving into
tHen not only is this not about you.
bUt you should probably just
kEep
iT
mOving

The eXquisite Pain, 3463

BaDFucKiNdeCisIonS
Fucking you would be a disservice to us both
And we both know better
Fucking you,
would lead to unexpected expectations
Call ...waiting
Waiting to call
to text
to see what's next, what's left after the smoke of moan signals
and soul mixing disintegrates into the air,
I would lose control
I admit to that.
Fucking you ain't gonna be no kick back, I might start to over think some shit and come up with sudden questions
and too many 'what you doing's' to stay safe guarded. Fucking you is gonna rattle my alarm system.
I need to know where your head's at and I don't mean the flick of your tongue
I mean us: where is our alignment?
What are we doing because the person I'm screwing (as momma would say)
needs to be bold enough to ACT in his truth without wavering.
Fucking you is just going to confuse these things.
It would be an insult to our potential.
An assault on our time clocks.
Every breath we take is getting us closer to death and I'd
rather not waste what I have left on a man who just wants my crawl space
open on his bed.
Make me know I'm not an option on a cross contaminated plate.
Rather,
I am the muthafuckin muse.
The liaison, the reason and the sum of things.
I Am
        The love, the one,
                The sun dance in your darkest downturns.

I'm a guiding light,
> The blind in your sight and the sight in your blind.

Fucking you would be a disservice to every place our minds could go to complete each other's unstructured sentences.
I can be your subject
And you can be my predicate
And we can plant kisses on paper as if we the ink in words
Like we the definition in words
Like we are letters standing in cursive formation, connected and hooked from one to the other,
as if we were rhythm and blues notes sitting
> in defiance to staccato,
> between black and white lines,
> a love jones ending – beginning with learning until we are

loving each other
with perfect strikes.
Verbs and actions and shit.
I ain't got no more available time for bullshit, for lies and shit.
Matter a fact, you don't even have to want that shit.
Just step out of the way of the man who does!
Cause that's the one I want to keep close.
I don't want your ignored calls
or my confused feelings
And that's why fucking you would be a disservice to us both.

I am too much woman to be loved in a measuring cup.

The Chrysalis

Yes to you sis.

Yes to your vocal chords being open. Yes to your fingers and what they write. Yes to your prose, your poetry, your notes and one-liners. Yes to your jokes and Twitter threads, yes to that! Yes to the songs you pen and the ones you sing softly to yourself. Yes to what you share. Your art and what you wear, yes to your love of self. Yes to your love of your own well-being and your emotional competence. Yes to becoming visible. Yes to 'reclaiming your time' and power. Yes to healthy confrontation. Yes to emptying luggage and bags with each word you speak along the way. Yes to not living a lie. Yes to being done with empowering others to hurt you. Yes to taking your power Queen. Yes to your accomplishments, to your leveling up and your continuous rise. Yes to the fight and the dedication. To becoming renewed and free. Yes to releasing what does not serve you in white gloves. Yes to your healing sis. Yes to all of you and whatever it takes. And to those who are silent; who embrace the quiet and pick up their toys and go when it's time with no pushback that the masses could detect; yes to you.

Your (r) Evolution is personal and can start and restart at any time. It will never be too late to be renewed and demand results. Before you exit the current chrysalis, say yes to yourself.

Yes to you sis.

Put a Wing on It: Rambling from El Matador Beach

Jealousy sometimes camouflages itself as support, love, and light. As bewildering as it might be that someone you have a close relationship is jealous of you, it happens often. Envious people are takers. They can't help themselves because they need to remove something from you to gain a greater sense of self. The satisfaction comes from gaining access to your soul and having the power to manipulate it to their satisfaction. If a person gains control of your confidence, they are instantly empowered because there's a level of control shifted to their hands. They take one feather at a time from your wings until you're able to be molded into who they believe you should be to or for them. Their personal greatness is defined by how weak you are for them. Getting you in a position where you are compromising your values and integrity is like weight training for their fragile, little muscles.

When a person is struggling to live through their own insecurities and fears, shortcomings, and missteps, they sometimes only find fulfillment in the control of someone else. When you find yourself in a relationship with one of these people, you will experience a shift that attempts to tame you and forward your focus to their causes rather than your own. These types of folks tend to have very little control over virtually anything else in their lives. Jealousy is a dangerous drug often ingested in the stomachs of those who struggle to find a purpose in their actuality. They need to become principle to something, and unfortunately, that is sometimes another person.

It is all too possible to fall in love with a fly ass weight. This means the person (male or female) that you have entered a relationship with, has all your love but no wings, no feathers, and no ability to help you fly. No matter how hard you pull them in the direction of up, they will always bring you down. There are times when we meet and fall in love with people who can only offer us first base. As the relationship progresses, you start to see the ship isn't moving, and every time you cut the anchor free, another hindrance disrupts the motions of your partnership. Congratulations, this is falling in love with a flyweight. While it might 'look' good in pictures for onlookers, it feels like a punishment. That is because what happens when you put a dumbbell on a feather?

It hits the ground.

Some people don't understand when a person is trying to build with them. It's not always intentional; many of us were raised in an emotionless mode of survival, and it's the only way we know to be. The wrong person will see your attributes as hindrances to their personal greatness and trust me when I say this: a jealous person is always the wrong person. Anything interfering with personal growth is automatically opposition to the relationship.

No wing can fly above an anchor – gravity will not allow for it. You will need to decide for yourself what rope gets cut. Is it the one grounding your flight to the cement, or do you no longer seek to (be) fly?

Trust me, when I say releasing the hand that you are holding, snapping pictures with and looking good next to (also known as a WEIGHT) will open the sky up for you. The sidewalk will become a liftoff. You won't need to run. Just keep walking. You will be flying before you know it. Evict all negative energy with a smile and never turn around for them to catch back up to you. Fuck em and feed em' concrete! (Be) Fly sis.

Fly until you fly into someone already up there looking for you, and if you never do, fly until you reach the heavens.

Feel free to stop and catch your breath, but please, only eat the worms.

Don't wife them niggas.

WYFS
For Rheagan, 4.16.15

And when she walks, Darling-
Each step is a royal deal of the cards but

confuse her not with anything less

than Ace of Spade,
Queen of not getting played
Slaying demons and evil, mystic shit that can be turned over at any hand

"Is that 3 Jacks I see??!! Dismiss this shit and deal again!

Off with this peasantry!"

Confess your sins before you approach.

Be an altar of honesty.
A fruit from a legendary harvesting.
For she is a Warrior Queen
Foundations have been laid for her arrival

So, watch your fucking step!
Matter a fact,
don't step on her Robe, those

are globetrotting wings.

Imperial, sovereign things.
What chakra balancing brings

Scream, that were turned into sunshine

for half-empty glasses,

She could give classes on dancing circles around stress

in a little black dress because,

> *'Oh, how we mourn the*
>
> *dead idea that she couldn't pass any test.'*

Listen here,

This is a moon goddess, mmmk?!

Chief Operating Boss over the Beats by Day-She-Was-Born.
And she's still here!
Coloring in hues she created,
Hues of orange,

and red prisms of courage,
She's a powerhouse.

A Queen dressed in gowns made from galaxies

with trains that blow toward the horizon

Look into her eyes and you will see the Crown of Seven Lives.

A sister to the circumference of where freedom lies,

and the nucleus of where truth unfolds.
Ace of Spades baby,
Queen of Diamonds
This is the game she controls.

There is no broken,
Only the rise of the tides of Warrior strides,
High on these hills in heels so fly,

using the clouds as magic carpets. Dare to glance toward her light and you will undoubtedly be immersed

in the Rays of Earth.
The Rhea of Sunlight.
Sunshine,
Eyes of diamonds
Steps that resemble constellation patterns,
Warriors don't shake –
-unless it's something coming 'Off'.
Forward takeoff
Bags packed get left behind –
Luggage doesn't go where flies
Rhea.
…of sky smiles,
and clouds, waltzing for her entry
Be alarmed
Be amazed
Be surprised she made it when the rest thought her fall would be delicious.
Be in support of-
-Or denial about the depth of which her elevation navigates the skies…

Be aware when a Warrior refuses to be less than an Ace of Spades in a flawless dress,

And watch your fucking step when she arrives!

The (RE)Tired Red Cape: Rambling from the Lido Deck

So, when is the last time you removed your cape? Look behind you and check. It's either flying in the wind right now or resting at ease against the richness of your blackness. We don't get to remove these things that often, or at least I don't, so I am wondering for the women reading this, when is the last time you got to remove your superwoman cape? Do you ever send it off to be cleaned? Of course, you could do it at home, but if we are tasked with wearing these things, I would like to think a professional once over by a reputable dry-cleaning service would be afforded to us from time to time. But that's the catch-twenty-one now isn't it: to get it cleaned, we would have to remove the cape. I've yet to meet a black woman that didn't have the Cape of Black Valor adorning her back; it's like an African American tribal scarification.

I'm sure every woman has some form of a cape in her closet. We've all felt tasked with the title of superwoman or like we were holding everything together through our sometimes-weary muscles. But the difference between a white woman's superwoman title and a black woman's cape is quite grandiose. Someone is always looking to offer or create protection for a white woman, whether it's white men, BLACK MEN, feminism, the courts, etc.... There is space made for them to be soft and delicate; to make mistakes and find reform. Their tears are expected and coddled, even when they are complete bullshit.

It appears a white woman's superwoman cape is always at the dry cleaners and, God bless her, she never takes it there herself.

Black women are underrepresented, under-protected, and misunderstood, and we are incarcerated twice as much as white women. Our doctors don't even take our health concerns seriously, as evidenced by Serena Williams. After a taxing birthing experience, Serena had to summons the wind beneath her cape and force her doctors to fully examine her. They would go on to discover several blood clots in her lungs. She almost died, and many black women with less money, fame, KNOWLEDGE, and healthcare in similar situations do die. If we dare remove our capes, we might as well sign our death certificate figuratively, if not literally. A black woman's cape is always attached to the back of whatever she wears from formal, custom gowns to pajamas and period panties. There is no off switch; we are always on. You don't get the title of superwoman because you get up and go to work every day. You get it because YOU are work every day. We are constantly working to finesse every barrier against us, and we hardly travel alone. There's family, friends, lovers, and children who often depend on us. Our lives are peppered with the recurring theme of "if not us, then who?" You've seen the memes that say, "black women be like fuck it, I'll do it," right?

Our grind goes so far beyond ourselves and even our families that remembering how and when to put ourselves first must be a conscious, dedicated act. We are constantly combating the idea that we should settle for whatever we can get from work to love. We toggle the fine line between remaining true to ourselves and conforming in society to get to the spaces we want to occupy. Then, of course, there is the 'angry black woman' syndrome that I personally believe is bullshit. You know what the problem with that is? It suggests we don't have the right to have feelings, anger included. It's as if passion is above our reach, and if we don't fit into the cookie-cutter mold of how other folks think we should handle our emotions, we are assumed to be loud and uncontrollable. But aren't we still daughters, mothers, grandmothers, and aunties? We are women who carry a generation of recipes, remedies and curses all in the same bosom. We're survivors, fearlessly heading our households through smudges and living room altars. We are the women tasked with moving forward after burying our kings and, too often, our children. Not a lick of slander nor a hint of the footprints left behind those who trespassed against us has or will stop us from reaching our ultimate greatness. Hell, we should be angry! This is a journey of setting intentions that is exhausting sometimes.

As much as it is beautiful and enlightening, it can be draining.

It is through these threads that our capes are created.

Rosa Parks didn't stay seated because she had plans to become the face of desegregation. She was admittedly tired of playing that psychologically abusive game where black women (people) didn't deserve the same basic human rights and treatments as white people. It was a cape she was tired of wearing. In our daily lives, black women are wearing the capes of many colors. We could have walk-in closets dedicated to the various wind-catchers we can be found wearing on any given day. The right woman on the right day might be wearing more than one. It's not one size fits all, but absolutely all sizes have a fit. I believe the rise in self-care events and activities, black yoga and herbal specialists, sound healers and tarot readers is due in part to black women realizing how many of us are walking around, bent over, spine deforming, emotions contorting, and sight muddled by a foggy haze all because we have been wearing these capes, nonstop. We've taken no breaks from being superwoman; our capes spend no time at the cleaners and are hardly found anywhere aside from attached to our backs. The load will be heavier this way.

We need to give ourselves the same permissions as white women have afforded their reflections. They don't wear their capes all the time, and someone else runs them to the cleaners on their behalf. They kick their feet up in Louboutin's, wipe, and reshape their brows and turn their unbothered lamps on high shade. In the words of Notorious B.I.G., we need to "relax and take notes." It's time to catch up, Queens! Black women are undeniably changemakers and trendsetters, but we are still behind on this cape-less movement and it's time we afforded ourselves those same permissions. It's ok to not have all the answers or to not be able to internalize someone else's stress. Say no when your answer is really no. Don't obligate yourself to code-switching and trying to have everything together all the time. Instead, be ok with taking that cape off, stretching out your legs, and existing as you are. Do more of what makes you happy. Whether it's for an hour or for a year, it's necessary. And guess what: you get to decide for how long!

EpiloVe

There's a certain high vibration that I think most of us want to achieve when it comes to love and relationships. It is a space where trust, wisdom, and understanding are plenteous. Fear, argumentative communication, and self-serving decisions are unorthodox and absent. Loving someone requires patience with one's natural evolution and the acceptance of their present wholeness. They will be who they are until they are not; there is no molding you can do to another person. You shouldn't attempt to mold anyone anydamnway - mold makes everybody sick. All you can do is inspire each other, and that can be positively or negatively, but you'll never build-your-own fantasy person. No one else can determine when and how the other matures. Either stand in awe or leave in disappointment, but don't stick around envying the yester-you in folks. If they don't qualify for your love, let them go. But don't focus too much on the other person's shortcomings and not your own, or you might forget to grow. This is how the death of relationships begins. While discussing his marriage in an interview with Elliot Wilson (Tidal), Will Smith posed the question of whether the "seed and the soil are married," or are they "growing [as individuals] together, doing what they are supposed to do?" Companionship is not owed or due to you, nor will it erase your insecurities. Building love on a foundation of what one is doing for the other is guaranteed to be shaky terrains. The seed is not married to the soil, and it doesn't stop to check how the ground is behaving before it harvests a flower. In fact, its purpose is for harvest, and it acts on its own accord. In partnership with the soil, this yields promising results. The soil works similarly. It transfers nutrients and promotes growth, regardless of the condition of the seed. A broken bulb or cracked ground doesn't mean a garden can't be produced. But a dead seed or dried soil will cause a considerable hindrance to continued growth. If you want to prosper as a couple, you both have to know how to flourish as individuals. The idea of 50/50 was always dangerous and ill-informed. Both parties should bring 100% to the table; the yield is at least 200%. So, where are you today? In a flower garden or flowering a cemetery? As for me. I'm at the window seat with my shades on, focused on my personal elevation. The altitude is high; forty-one thousand feet above it all. And I'm not coming down anymore. The next person will have to meet me in the sky.

Affirmational Ingredient List

      I am too much woman to be loved via any of the following:
- a measuring cup
- a teaspoon
- a tablespoon
- anything that measures weight
                -an action-less sentence spoken in longing ears
- a cereal bowl
- a milk carton side
- a pop can
- a line of coke
- a puff of blunt
- a glass half empty
- anything that measures weight
        -an action-less sentence spoken towards yearning eyes
- a plastic spork
- a knife and fork
- a closed book
- a half completed chapter
- a bunch of metaphoric bullshit
- a poem
- a platinum plaque
- anything that measures weight
        -an action-less sentence spoken against a beating heart
- a lie
- a mystery clouded with confusion
- a dipstick
- an oil change

-a dead end street

- an ant farm

- a short flight

-an orgasm

-head

- doggy style love letters because they don't produce fairytale endings

- anything that measures weight

    -an action-less sentence spoken for no fucking reason.

  I am too much woman to be loved via a measuring cup.

  Weighed out on a table scale, fed scaled down, bitten into portions of mold covered love in bits and pieces, it may sound astonishing, but

I DESERVE love not found CLINGING to the surfaces of teaspoons.

Dedications

This book is dedicated to the free spirited, blackity black black women who weren't born to be tied down, held back or loved improperly, and still believes there is a lover out there who will love her higher than he found her. To the women who love the wrong people and the women who don't understand those who they attract: just as bees are attracted to honey, people come to you to drink from your well and get full. Don't let them make you think something is wrong with you. Just be more intentional about whose glass you will offer a fill. And never pour into anyone who is not pouring back into you!!!!

"To the grandmothers
who were first mothers
and once daughters
or better yet,
black women,
Thank you
for sticking around long enough to leave us with the ability to keep swimming."

To Zora Neale Hurston – My doppelganger. Spiritual ancestor in many ways. I thank you Zora, for your contributions to black literature. You are the epitome of standing in your truth and you took the hits for it. It is because of you that I freely write about love, pain and triumph.

To my favorite foursome: my grandmother, mother, and two aunts - Netria, Alvetrice, Millie, and Jessie Ruth - the four women who raised me, who taught me what it meant to be a woman in four parts. Women whose love experiences made more sense the older I became. I love you all so much. I really do. I speak for you as I do myself.

Anitra (Nitro) & Queen B. – My journey began with the two of you. You were two of THE brightest lights at The Cozy. My life was incredibly blessed to have been able to become close sisterfriends with you both. I dedicate this book to the love you wanted, deserved and especially the love you gave. I will spend the rest of my life missing you and I will never let your flames burn out. I love you. Thank you.

Reaux & Robiniee – My Earth Angels. For you, I write as well. I love you, for life. For loving quirky, lil ole' me but mostly, for being incredibly dope human beings.

***

Thank you for reading! Now that you've made it to the end, I hope you have found a new beginning to your personal story and can see how I wrote this book and final poem as a way of paying homage to all of you. All of us.

The black women who love.

Thank you Queens.

Intergalactic, Unapologetically Black Women I Know:
I know stars
Real life
Astronomical objects, deserving of affectionate support
And endless love
I know stellar pieces of galaxy that have floated to earth
Gracing the land with illumination
They say most stars can't be seen,
But I've witnessed some of the brightest universal productions
Right off the cusp of 465
Alive with bright eyes, they awaken morning risings with coffee conversations across news stations,
I know stars that don't stop cooking.
Hips twisted in the kitchen, watch her fly.
Legendary stars that take over the daytime and could steal the moonshine from the night.
I'm telling you, I know real life stars.
Spectrums with colors blossoming from melanated cheekbones.
The song singing types that pack out Jazz Kitchens on cold winter nights.
Batting mink lashes next to the birdie sitting on the windowsill smoking a peace pipe,
The type to look death in the eye and say "not me tonight",
The Ph.D. types,
Trappin out the brick and mortar,
then bending corners in RAM 150, I know stars that ain't shifty and flighty,
They gifted and mighty in spite of the opposition.
While others are waiting on dusk to settle to start their wishes,
I get a cluster of cheek kisses from Nova's so full of power that they can't be referred to without the Super.
This ain't about no rhyme scheme but homage paying to the Queens I know.
To the QUEEN I still know.
Watch your fucking step.
These are wives to dreams,

Mothers to miracles,
Divas to Runways,
Healers to places and spaces that they designated as their own,
moving like a blast of Nitro from The Sunset to sunrise.
Beaded jewelry adorned from their waistline to the creases of their eyes.
They are prized possessions; these stars are. They are prized possessions and should be treated as if one upward turn from their lips can get you lifted to the next level.
Smart home, long hair,
Dark car, don't care,
These women are stars.
I know real life stars yo!
Peaches that birth Januaries
Doulas, dancers and visionaries...
Creators of creations that save lives.
Jazzy stars with melodic voices that can switch from song to poem,
Centering Urban Wellness from work to home,
Document experts that could run the tech world on their own.
Using words as their weapons like M'reld gemstones.
A dimension of Rebelles and rebellions, activists and hellions, we-came-to-bring-the-pain-
So,
Inhale the perfume and be amazed
Witness the shine and blink their reflection for days.
See what I am in constant amaze from.
What fuels my run sometimes when the road gets lonely as one.
I know stars.
In real life.
All in a constant elevation as if synchronized swimming . . .
I know stars in real life
And they have all taken on the shape of the most incredible black women.

Final Thought: Somewhere, On Eugene Street, Sitting on a Porch.

Life is short.

And all of it, from the food we eat to the days we are here, is temporary. The only permanent is death.

Love as best as you can, and when you think you're great at it, love better. But know that it starts within yourself. You will never get someone to love you out of your personal demons and you'll never love anyone well as long those demons are with you. But it's all temporary. Get rid of it. Seek healing. Growth. Change. Evolution. Personal revolution.

And then love the next person or the one who sticks around through it all, as though you might not be able to love past the next second.

~*januarie*, 4112019230PM

About the Author

For over a decade, Januarie York has been carving her own lane in poetry, writing and performance art. Januarie is a freelance writer, published author & poet who, in addition to performing original poetry, has produced several of her own spoken word theatrical shows that focus on uplifting and inspiring women. A recent graduate with her Bachelor's in Criminal Justice, she is currently pursuing her Master's in Positive Psychology.

Januarie has released two spoken word albums, one chapbook of poetry, runs an online magazine publication called, "LiT Magazine" and currently operates her own blog, "The I Is Never Silent". She has also acted in several plays including "Wizer of Oz" and "For Colored Girls Only, for which she wrote two original poems for. She resides in Indianapolis, IN, where in addition to curating poetry shows, she has created several community healing events and works with the 46208-based organization "The Learning Tree." She has worked with the Asante Children's Theater, Eskenazi Hospital, IU Health, Visit Indy, Indianapolis Central Library and the Fair Housing Act of Indiana to name a few.

www.ingramcontent.com/pod-product-compliance
Lightning Source LLC
LaVergne TN
LVHW011844060526
838200LV00054B/4162